Haggai & Malachi
At His Feet Studies

By Hope A. Blanton and Christine B. Gordon

Contents

How to Use This Study

There is no right way to lead a Bible study. Every Bible study group is made up of different types of people with various needs and dynamics. These are some suggestions that might be helpful when using At His Feet Studies. Read it through. Use what you want. Forget the rest. We're glad you're here.

A different approach to a familiar method

As with many Bible studies you're familiar with, we follow a pattern of observation, interpretation, and application, but the presentation may be a little different than what you're used to. Instead of bouncing between those three tasks, we group them.

First, you will read a biblical passage, and using the Observation Questions, you'll note the people mentioned, terms used, commands given, actions taken, and so on. This is arguably the most important step, as the Word of God itself is powerful and active.

In the next section, you will interpret the biblical passage with help from seminary-trained Chris. The Interpretation section is written in the style of most commentaries, offering a verse-by-verse explanation of the biblical passage. This section is rooted in study of the original language and multiple sources, including commentaries, original language helps, sermons, theological treatises, and personal conversations with seminary professors.

Finally, you will apply the biblical text to your life, assisted by licensed therapist Hope and her heart-engaging Reflection Questions.

In this way, you will read, interpret, and then reflect on a larger passage as a whole, keeping the words and message in their context.

What do I do each day?

You can read through and complete the entire study in one sitting or break it up. If you'd like to spread out your preparation a bit more, break it into three days: On day 1, read the biblical passage and complete the Observation Questions. On day 2, read the Interpretation section. On day 3, complete the Reflection Questions. You could even add a day 4 and attempt to memorize or simply meditate on the focus verse and/or write down your thoughts in the space for "Reflections, curiosities, frustrations."

How do I lead a group through this study?

It is always a good idea to read through the biblical passage out loud at the beginning of your time together. After reading the Scripture aloud, choose one or two Observation Questions and answer them as a group.

If most of your group has had a chance to read the Interpretation section on their own, ask them what stood out to them in that section and talk through parts of the commentary they may have highlighted. If you are leading a group with participants who have not had the time to read through the Interpretation section on their own, take the time to read it out loud as a group before asking this question.

Next, choose three or four of your favorite Reflection Questions and allow time for everyone who would like to offer their answers. These questions are written with the aim of both engaging your own heart and also engaging one another's hearts as you study together.

If you have the time, do all of the above *and* walk through all of the Reflection Questions. If you'd like, you could ask the group what questions or frustrations arose during their study.

Want an extra challenge?

Issue the challenge to your group to memorize the focus verse and say it together when you reconvene.

Questions? Reach out!

We would love to hear from you. Write to us at athisfeetstudies@gmail.com.

A Note on How to Read the Prophets

Though they are a treasure trove within God's Word, the prophets are often left untouched by believers in the twenty-first century. People who have never had the opportunity to study the prophets or had help to do so often find these books intimidating and inaccessible. May we offer four suggestions that will help you as you read this type of biblical genre:

1. **Remember the context.** The complex names and unfamiliar dating systems found in the prophets would have made sense to those receiving the original message. Read the text with the original hearers in mind, including their historical and cultural context, which is most easily found from other sources like a study Bible (or our commentary). Try to put yourself in their shoes and hear what they would have heard first before attempting to walk the passage's principles or truths back over the bridge to your own time, place, and culture.

2. **Look for the now and the later.** The prophets were speaking to their contemporaries, but the fullness of what their prophecies anticipated were often broader than what we immediately see. Look for ultimate fulfillments later in history. For example, Christ is often the ultimate fulfillment of temple prophecies.

3. **Consider the role of the prophet.** These men acted as God's mouthpieces mostly to remind Israel of the covenant promises God had made and their need to live in light of those promises. The prophets spoke to a nation chosen by God to be ruled by him specifically. No political equivalent to Israel now exists. Instead,

with the coming of the Holy Spirit, the people of God now represent all ethnicities and nations.

4. Look for New Testament references to the prophets. Jesus quoted or alluded to the prophets almost twenty times, Paul more than fifty times. New Testament saints saw their stories in continuity with the story the prophets were telling. Paul quoted the Old Testament repeatedly because his life was a continuation of God's promise to his people.

Take your time, and ask the Spirit for his help. There are riches contained in the prophetic books. They are worth finding.

Why study Haggai and Malachi together?

Haggai prophesied around 520 B.C., and Malachi followed sometime between 440 and 400 B.C. We've combined these two prophets because of their similar themes, which center around the temple and the worship taking place there. By studying these two prophets together rather than separately—sinking into their shared historical and cultural context—we get a fuller picture of God speaking to his people over time and a better understanding of the text. We see the spiritual state of Israel over the generations and their response—or lack thereof—to God's Word. We see how they did respond to Haggai's preaching but then had become sloppy in their worship by Malachi's day. We also see ourselves and our fickle hearts mirrored in the people of Israel during this little chunk of their history. May the same Spirit who roused the hearts of these men and women rouse our hearts as we study this ancient text.

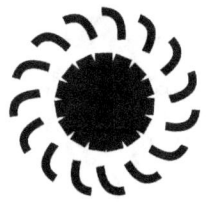

Study 1

This House Lies in Ruins

Read the entire Book of Haggai

Our Lord spoke to his people through Haggai during a difficult time in Israel's history. God's people were not living in their own land or anywhere near their beloved temple where they could meet with God. Because of generations of sin, God allowed another nation to attack Israel. Jerusalem, the city of David and home to Solomon's temple, had been destroyed by the Babylonians (a large and brutal empire whose people worshipped multiple gods) in the year 586 B.C. With the destruction of God's dwelling place, the temple, Israel probably feared that God had abandoned them altogether because of their sin (Lamentations 5:22). There was no longer any physical sign of God's presence among them. Not only that, most of the nation of Israel was taken away into captivity by the Babylonians, who were later captured themselves by the Persians. Israel lived in exile, oppressed, away from their homeland and their temple, defeated.

Almost fifty years passed between that destruction and the day the first of the exiled Israelites walked back into the city. When Cyrus of Persia issued the decree to return to Jerusalem and build the temple (around 538 B.C., see Ezra 1), a number of Israelites made the five-hundred-mile journey back. Very few of the people who had lived in or near the city were even alive anymore. Multiple generations had lived their entire lives in Babylon with no memory or experience of life in the city of David and a functional temple where God dwelt. They had never experienced worship at the temple where God had promised to meet with his people.

Though the temple was in ruins, the priests gave burnt offerings on an altar and celebrated various feasts as prescribed by God's law (Ezra 3). The people were able to restore a large part of the temple, an accomplishment that was loudly celebrated with trumpets, cymbals, and shouting. But when opposition came from their enemies, building stopped. Ezra 4:24 reads, "Then the work on the house of God that is in Jerusalem stopped, and it ceased until the second year of the reign of Darius king of Persia." In this book, Haggai addressed the Jews who had returned after exile in order to motivate them to renew their work on God's temple.

Re-read Haggai 1:1–11

Observation Questions

1. List the names of the people mentioned in Haggai 1:1 and any information written about them.

2. According to Haggai 1:2–4 and the last part of Haggai 1:9, what was God upset about? According to Haggai 1:7–8, what does he want the people to do about it?

3. What are the consequences for the people of God for leaving the temple unfinished (Haggai 1:5–6 and 1:10–11)?

Interpretation

Haggai 1:1. The specificity of the day given helps to authenticate the Book of Haggai. The "first day" of the month was significant in that Israelites would have been celebrating a feast day, an observation of the new moon, as commanded in Numbers 28:11 and referred to in Psalm 81:3, "Blow the trumpet at the new moon, at the full moon, on our feast day." This feast day would have included animal, grain, and drink offerings, as well as rejoicing, music, and time away from the fields.

We know very little about Haggai, the man, except that he was a prophet of the Lord. Zerubbabel we know more about. He was the grandson of King Jehoiachin who had been taken to Babylon in 597 B.C., and he was next in line to the throne of David. He was the ruler who led the first group of exiles back to Jerusalem around 538 B.C. Because Zerubbabel's authority was held under the Persian king (the Persians conquered the Babylonians and took over their empire), he did not have full sovereignty over the people of Israel. Joshua, the other leader mentioned in the first verse of this book, was of the Levite tribe and a priest, which meant he was responsible for the proper offering of sacrifices to God. Zerubbabel and Joshua served as the civil and religious leaders for Israelites who had returned to Judea, the area including Jerusalem and its surroundings.

Haggai 1:2. We can assume that the word of the Lord came through Haggai to both Joshua and Zerubbabel together, probably during an official visit between the two. The emperor of Persia was outwardly in charge of the political system in which these two men worked. But Haggai named God as "the LORD of hosts," the one in charge of angel armies and ultimately Persia as well. Notice how God referred to the returned Israelites—"these people." This was a rebuke to them, as God usually referred to "my people" when he spoke lovingly to Israel.

Returned Israelites had been living in Jerusalem and Judah for fifteen years since Cyrus's decree. And yet, even the foundation of God's house had not yet been totally repaired since the work was stopped by opposition. Why not? The people felt, "the time has not yet come." God's house was not their priority because *he* was not their first priority. Instead of working on the temple, they had been working on their own houses. Their first concern was their own interests, and working on God's house felt inconvenient.

Haggai 1:3–4. Haggai first addressed the leaders, and then he turned to the people, probably those gathered to celebrate the holy first day of the month. The temple was where the Lord dwelt; it was where he came near to his people. The Israelites understood God couldn't be contained to a building, but they also knew his house was the "outward form of the real presence of the Lord among his people."[1] A refusal to build the temple was a statement that the people didn't care about God's presence. To reject his house was to reject him. They were essentially saying to God, "We don't need you."

It was not as if the people of Israel didn't have time to do any work. Their own houses were not only finished but apparently were being decorated with some sort of paneling. It may have been that the governor's house was being adorned similarly to former kingly palaces. The people had placed their own comfort and even luxury above the finishing of the place where they could experience God's presence, a place that was a means of grace.

We can easily wag our fingers at these brothers and sisters, but some of us act in similar ways. The temptation to prioritize our own comfort above God's kingdom—specifically in the ways we spend our money and use our other resources—is reinforced by our own western culture. Jesus said, "Do not lay up for yourselves treasures on earth, where moth and rust destroy and where thieves break in and steal, but lay up for yourselves treasures in heaven, where neither moth nor rust destroys and where thieves do not break in and steal. For where your treasure is, there your heart will be also" (Matthew 6:19–21). We must ask God to show us the places in our own hearts where we have the same confusion in priorities as the Israelites did.

Haggai 1:5–7. Here we see the first instance of the word "consider," which is derived from the word meaning "heart" and could also be translated as "set your heart upon," "see," or "know." God was telling these Israelites, "Slow down and think about what you've been experiencing. Reflect upon the current situation; you do not have what you need. You work hard in the fields, but they don't produce. You eat food every day, but you're still hungry. You wear clothes, but you're not warm. You hire yourself out to work extra hours, but you're still behind."

In verse 7 we get that same word again, "consider." Allow your inner person, your soul, to see the truth.[2]

Haggai 1:8–9. This word was spoken through Haggai in the sixth month. The Israelites would have just harvested their grain a couple of months before and would have still had images of the disappointing yields in their minds. At this point the Lord had the attention of his people. The prescription for their problems was then revealed: They were to build his temple. This was not a new command but one they had known about for many years and had been postponing and putting off until the "right time" revealed itself. God knew waiting for the exact "right time" was an insincere excuse and called them to obey now.

It was customary to build walls of both wood and stone in order to protect against earthquake damage. The hills around Jerusalem were covered in forests, and stone still left from the destruction of the temple was probably lying around, providing what was needed for building.

If his people would build by faith, God would do two things: He would (1) "take pleasure" in the house and (2) he would "be glorified." He would take pleasure, meaning he would receive their efforts at building his house as an acceptable sacrifice, just as he might accept a burnt offering given by a priest. God would also "be glorified" in their building of the temple. Unlike some other instances in the prophets where God was honored by bringing destruction to those who were against him, glory would come in the form of faithful love and tenderness toward his people.

Having given them the circumstances to consider—their lack of satisfaction along with their lack of obedience in building the temple—God addressed the problem plainly in verse 9. It's as if he were saying, "Things aren't going well for you because you're ignoring my house and prioritizing yours." Though they had already finished building their houses, they continued to spend their money and time on them while the temple lay in ruins.

Haggai 1:10–11. Grain, wine, and oil were the three most important products of the Israelites' farms. They were the products that overflowed in a time of blessing, and their firstfruits were to be given to the Lord (Deuteronomy 18:4). Without regular yields of these staple crops, the economy of Israel fell apart. It was God who had been frustrating their efforts, denying them the dew and rain that would have prevented the drying of crops in the August and September heat. It was God who sent a drought.

No matter how hard they worked, these men and women didn't have enough. This is the picture of futility and dissatisfaction. They used their lack to justify delaying work on the temple, but God said it was the other way around: their lack was a direct consequence of their disobedience in refusing to put the temple first. We need to be careful as we apply this story: It is not a formula for getting what we want or even for avoiding pain. Instead, God wanted them to trust and depend on him, no matter what he asked. He wants the same of us. He calls us all to obedience out of our love for him, no matter the outcome.

When Jesus took on flesh and entered our world, the fullness of God dwelt among us—something greater than the temple had come! We no longer needed a building to know God's special presence. Though we no longer have a temple to build, we do have a church to grow. The equivalent of the Old Testament's temple is not a church building but the church itself—God's people in whom he now dwells by his Spirit. And the command for us is not physically to build a place for God to dwell but to make disciples. We must make God's mission our first priority. As Jesus said in Matthew 6:33, "But seek first the kingdom of God and his righteousness, and all these things will be added to you."

Reflection Questions

4. The temple was a tangible sign for the Israelites of meeting with and engaging with God's presence. Why do you think this started to seem less important to them?

5. Are you surprised at the consequences God gave the Israelites to get their attention? When do you feel he has done this for you?

6. God tells his people that he would experience pleasure and be glorified by the rebuilding of the temple, meaning that the obedience of his people has an effect on him. What does this show us about the character of God?

7. The modern day temple is the church of believers. What about "building" his church feels hard for you to prioritize? Why?

8. While it will look different for each believer, what does it look like practically to seek God's kingdom over your own priorities? How can you pray for God to bring his kingdom and your concerns more in sync?

Focus verse

Thus says the LORD of hosts: Consider your ways. Go up to the hills and bring wood and build the house, that I may take pleasure in it and I may be glorified, says the LORD.

Haggai 1:7–8

Reflections, curiosities, frustrations:

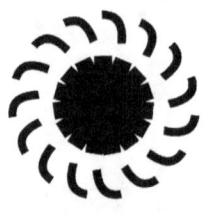

Study 2

Work, for I Am with You

Read Haggai 1:12–2:9

Observation Questions

1. In Haggai 1:13, what did the Lord say to his people through Haggai? What resulted from this in Haggai 1:14?

2. In Haggai 2:3, the Lord speaks through Haggai to Zerubbabel, Joshua, and the remnant of the people and asks three questions. What are they?

3. In Haggai 2:9 what does the Lord say about this new temple? What does he say he is going to do?

Interpretation

Zerubbabel, the governmental authority; Joshua, the religious authority; and all the people had just listened to a rebuke from God for their neglect of the temple while their houses were continually improved. Don't miss what happens next.

Haggai 1:12. In verse 12 we read that the people "obeyed the voice of the Lord their God." In that little phrase is a supernatural work. In the majority of the accounts we read of prophets in the Old Testament speaking for God, the people's response is much different than this. Israel was often a "stiff-necked people"

(Exodus 32:9) who "would not listen" (2 Kings 17:14). The fact that they both heard and acted implies repentance, something that does not happen without the work of the Holy Spirit. The people also "feared the LORD," meaning they revered him with the respect and worship deserved by their Creator. This is the opposite of the apathy that characterized them before the destruction of Jerusalem.

In Haggai 1:2, God referred to those in Judah as "these people," a distant and punishing title, but now they are called "the remnant of the people." This applied both to those who never left Jerusalem and its surrounding area after the Babylonians destroyed the city and to those who returned to Jerusalem when Cyrus gave them permission. Their response to God shows them to be the true Israel—a true remnant. These brothers' and sisters' faithfulness is what marks them as the remnant, those belonging to God and his covenant.

Haggai 1:13–15. Immediately after the people began the work, God spoke a word of encouragement to them. It's almost as if he were just waiting to comfort them, waiting to strengthen and embolden them at their first movement toward obedience. But it was not only words he gave to his people in order to equip and enable them to do what he asked. The same people he asked to build the house he also empowered to build the house. The Lord "stirred up," meaning he "woke up" or "set in motion," the spirits of Zerubbabel, Joshua, and all the people.

This was not the first time God had "stirred up" his people for obedience. The first wave of exiles written about in the Book of Ezra were also responding to God's work. Ezra 1:5 reads, "Then rose up the heads of the fathers' houses of Judah and Benjamin, and the priests and the Levites, everyone whose spirit God had stirred to go up to rebuild the house of the LORD that is in Jerusalem." From the very first Israelites who returned to Jerusalem, God had been at work empowering and inspiring his people. Did the Israelites work when they returned? Yes. Was God at work in them to enable their work? Absolutely. Our work is always a response to God moving first.

The "Lord of Hosts" is a title that occurs frequently in the Old Testament. "Hosts" refers to armies, meaning angel armies—which is just what it sounds like, large armies of angels. While other nations were always a threat to tiny, weak Israel, their God was the commander of a supernatural army. This powerful God was as great in his love as he was in his might. He graciously gave his people a willingness to work, that he might dwell with them in the temple. Though his work may look different, the Holy Spirit is the same enabler and encourager for us in our work to build the kingdom as he was for Israel in their work to build the temple.

Why did it take twenty-three days for work to begin on the temple once the people heard and repented? First, plans had to be made for the giant work of fixing the foundation and building on top of it. In addition, the sixth month was the month of harvest, and ripe crops do not wait for anyone. The Feast of Tabernacles, during which no work could have taken place, would also have fallen during these days.

Haggai 2:1. Another four weeks went by as the people began to repair the temple. As all Israel near Jerusalem came for the Feast of Tabernacles (also called the Feast of Booths), a few things probably occurred. First, there would have been a joint remembrance, as there always was, of Israel's life in Egypt and how God brought them out of slavery in the Exodus. The people would have built and lived in booths for seven days to commemorate this huge event in their history. This would have brought to mind the magnificent temple of Solomon, which was dedicated on the Feast of Tabernacles so many years before. For those toiling to build without the endless resources of workers, wood, and gold Solomon had access to, remembering his temple while looking at theirs even after a month of work was probably very depressing. Those who traveled to Jerusalem for the feast probably felt the same way as they saw so little progress. To add to their discouragement, the Feast of Tabernacles was usually a time of great rejoicing for the bounty of the harvest, but the harvest was not plentiful that year. God's people were in danger of being swallowed by dismay.

Haggai 2:2–3. Like a compassionate father watching his children attempt a difficult task, just waiting to encourage them along the way, God knew what his people needed. Notice he didn't start by telling them what to do. First, God met the people where they were. In modern terms he asked them, "Did any of you see Solomon's temple? Does this one look like that one did? It sure looks discouraging, doesn't it?" God validated their feelings. The new temple at this point did not look like the old.

For Israel, it must have seemed that their work was futile. They did not have what they needed to make the temple magnificent as it had been. For the church, the people of God in a New Testament era, our work in building the church can often feel the same way. We may not have the money or other resources we think we need to reach people with the good news of Jesus or teach them how to live for him. The church itself often looks like it's a hot mess compared to what we read about in the Book of Acts or Paul's letters. But God knows the encouragement we need. He speaks courage to us as he did to Israel.

Haggai 2:4–5. Be strong, be strong, be strong. And work, for I am with you. These were the commands God gave to Israel as they looked at the outwardly plain, small results of their work. He wanted their focus to be not on their ability or resources but on his ability and resources. The key was not their faithfulness but his. Their hope was found not in their energy, organization, or commitment but in his promise. Just as he had been with them as they came out of Egypt, so his Spirit was with them still. Just as he had guided and protected them in the Exodus, so he would do the same in the building of the temple.

The victory in the world would be won by the God of angel armies. His war chest would be filled with the precious things of the nations.[1] At this point, Haggai was not speaking of things that would happen immediately. Don't miss the "in a little while" of verse 6, remembering that "with the Lord a day is like a thousand years and a thousand years are like a day" (2 Peter 3:8). The temple would be made beautiful by God at the right time. This was the physical temple he was speaking of, but it was not only that; Haggai was beginning to speak of a future temple as well.

Haggai 2:8–9. All the gold and silver of the world ultimately belongs to God. He could put it where he wanted and use it as he wished, including in his temple. But what would eventually be the temple was greater than any earthly precious metal. Whatever amount of God's presence had been experienced in the former temple of Solomon would be far exceeded by the fullness of God that came in Christ. In Christ, God came even nearer to his people.

We, the church, are the current temple where God dwells. We may look about as unadorned and unimpressive as the ruined temple must have looked to the Israelites when trying to rebuild. We are often undisciplined, slow, awkward, and embarrassing. Our efforts at telling the news of Jesus or training people in his Word can "seem as nothing." But God doesn't give up on what he starts. He is faithful to finish the work he began, both in individuals and throughout the worldwide church. We must move our hopes from our own weak efforts and invest them in God's power and promises. We must hear him say to us as he did to Israel, "Be strong and work, for I am with you."

God has proved himself faithful to his promises. The fact that the New Testament church exists hundreds of years later and has reached the United States, the United Kingdom, China, Peru, South Africa, and other lands hardly known at the time when Haggai was speaking God's Word is evidence that God is continuing to do what he promised. His dwelling place, his church, continues to grow. And as all of the nations parade into the new heavens and new earth one day, we can be sure they will bring with them all their treasures, all for the glory of God as he dwells with his people.

Reflection Questions

4. The people heard the message from Haggai and repented and embraced what the Lord was saying to them, which revealed them as God's people. When have you seen the similar act of repentance among God's people?

5. After they had repented God came in with words of comfort and encouragement. Does that surprise you? Why do you think God did that?

6. God comforted his people, encouraged them, empowered them to start the work, and gave them the ability to carry it out, showing his faithfulness to what he was asking them to do. How have you found this to be true of him in your own life?

7. As they built the temple they felt discouraged that they didn't have access to the resources they needed to restore it in the way they wanted to. We can often feel that way with the modern church. When have you felt that type of discouragement about resources when it comes to "building up" the church as we seek to make disciples?

8. The fact that you are even sitting here today doing this study on Haggai and Malachi shows that God's faithfulness to his people from this moment in history so long ago has extended all the way to you. What is your reaction to that thought?

Focus verse

Yet now be strong, O Zerubbabel, declares the LORD. Be strong, O Joshua, son of Jehozadak, the high priest. Be strong, all you people of the land, declares the LORD. Work, for I am with you, declares the LORD of hosts, according to the covenant that I made with you when you came out of Egypt. My Spirit remains in your midst. Fear not.

Haggai 2:4–5

Reflections, curiosities, frustrations:

Study 3

I Have Chosen You

Read Haggai 2:10–23

Observation Questions

1. In Haggai 2:11–14, what questions did the Lord and Haggai ask the priests? What were the priests' answers?

2. In Haggai 2:15–19, what did the Lord say happened to the people's things before they started to rebuild the temple? What did he say would happen from this point going forward now that the foundation of the temple was laid?

3. In Haggai 2:20–23, what did the Lord say he was going to do on behalf of Zerubbabel?

Interpretation

Haggai 2:10. It had been exactly three months since the remnant of Israel began working to rebuild the temple. It had also been two months since God's last encouragement to "Be strong" and "Work." The ninth month was the time of year for sowing seed, when all Israel would have exercised what power they had by planting and by praying for God to bless the crops. Remember that for years, they'd been experiencing only 50 percent yields. God was reminding them why they'd had such a shortage, and why it would now be different.

Had the Israelites done something wrong? It almost seems here as if they were being rebuked once more by the prophet. Actually, this was the day they finished the foundation of the temple, a great accomplishment and milestone. This was a day to be celebrated and a time to remember their history. So many of God's words to Israel contain reminders of their past and his love. This day was both a sober reminder of the consequences of sin and a joyful looking forward to God's blessings in obedience.

Haggai 2:11–13. One of the responsibilities of priests in Israel was to explain the law to the people (Leviticus 10:10–11). Haggai was probably preaching in the temple, where the physical work of the priests would have been on display. God offered an object lesson to explain the importance of the temple and his presence.

Haggai asked about the possibility of holiness passing from meat to clothing to another food. The priests, who daily handled sacrifices as dictated by sacrificial law, would have answered this question easily. When giving meat sacrifices to God, anything the meat touched would become holy (Leviticus 6:25–27). So if the priest carried some of the meat in his clothing, the clothing would be holy. But if that clothing then touched something else, the holiness would not be passed on. In other words, holiness was only transmissible one time. It went from the sacrifice to one surface and then stopped.

Haggai then gave another scenario, this time including something unclean. The Levitical law was given by God in the Book of Leviticus to instruct the priests and people in how to handle sacrifices and other things in the temple and in Israel's life together. In it there was a whole category of objects and people that were considered unclean. This included all types of things from leprous people to certain creatures that creep on the ground (Leviticus 11 and following). Nothing unclean was allowed in the presence of a holy God, and people could become unclean by touching unclean things.

Touching a dead body was one way to become unclean that all Israel would have recognized (Numbers 19:11). Here Haggai was asking whether uncleanness can be transferred from one object to a person and then to another object. In other words, was uncleanness transmissible twice? "It does become unclean," the priests answered. Yes, uncleanness was more contagious than cleanness.

Haggai 2:14. Now comes the explanation for his object lesson. The people of Israel are unclean, and therefore what they touched was unclean. This would have included all of their sacrifices being offered to God. Though it's not explicitly named here, Haggai is implying that the unfinished temple itself is like a corpse that all of Israel keeps touching, rendering them unclean. The ruined temple stood in the city, a constant reminder of the people's apathy toward God. Continuing to offer sacrifices without finishing the temple was like trying to get God's blessing without welcoming his presence.

Haggai 2:15–17. Remember that on the day Haggai spoke these words, the people had just finished laying the temple foundation ("stone was placed upon stone"). Haggai was reminding them of their own history. Their crops had been yielding only half of what was expected. The grape harvest was even worse. God himself had interfered with the growth. "Blight" probably refers to excessive heat, and mildew would have come from excessive rain and humidity. Again, God used extremes of weather to imply that anything could be a tool in his hand. He could use any element of life to discipline his people.

God still disciplines his people today (Proverbs 3:12, Hebrews 12:6). In his discipline, he may prevent blessing or allow suffering. However, we are not prophets who hear God's decree as Haggai did. While we should consider our circumstances, as God asked the Israelites to do, we do not have the insight to label a certain circumstance as a discipline. Of course, we must consider our lives and repent of sin. However, it is a dangerous thing to decide for ourselves, for someone else, or for a nation that a certain type of suffering allowed by God is discipline for a certain action. We must avoid those who claim to be able to name such things.

An unmentioned voice in the mix at this point in Israel was that of Zechariah, who began his prophetic ministry to the same group of people about two months after Haggai. Zechariah had a very similar message for the remnant, though it was given in a series of visions. We can imagine these two men speaking for God in their very different ways and God using both to prompt action. Haggai began with a rebuke for the failure to build the temple. Zechariah's message began with a general call to turn back to God as the source and center of their lives, "The LORD was very angry with your fathers. Therefore say to them, Thus declares the LORD of hosts: Return to me, says the LORD of hosts, and I will return to you, says the LORD of hosts" (Zechariah 1:2–3). Both were appealing to God's people to obey their master.

Haggai 2:18–19. Here comes the good news. History was recounted, and the people were disciplined. Their hearts were changed, and their work on the temple continued. God had even more blessing to pour out on them. Remember that the ninth month would have been the time of year when seed would have been just planted. The people's answer to Haggai's question "Is the seed yet in the barn?" would have been "No." Nothing had been harvested yet. It was too early to even begin predicting a yield. And yet through Haggai, God promised a huge harvest. He would cause what quietly grew in the ground to multiply and overflow their barns. Again, it was as if God had been just waiting to bless, to give, to make Israel flourish.

God does not necessarily promise an overflowing physical or financial blessing to us today when we work to build his current dwelling place—the people of God. However, he does tell us in Matthew 6:33 that he will provide what we need such as food and clothing: "But seek first the kingdom of God and his righteousness, and all these things will be added to you." The posture of God's love now for his church is the same as it was for Israel. Put him first, serve his kingdom first, and he will take care of the rest.

God does promise oodles of spiritual blessing. James 4:8 reads, "Draw near to God, and he will draw near to you." Matthew 7:11 tells us, "If you then, who are evil, know how to give good gifts to your children, how much more will your Father who is in heaven give good things to those who ask him!" Psalm 31:19 promises, "Oh, how abundant is your goodness, which you have stored up for those who fear you." And 1 Peter 3:9 tells us, "Do not repay evil for evil or reviling for reviling, but on the contrary, bless, for to this you were called, that you may obtain a blessing."

Haggai 2:20–23. Haggai received a second message on the same day, this time for Zerubbabel, the governor of Judah. While God had promised to shake the nations to empty their pockets and put their treasures in his house (Haggai 2:7), here he is saying he will shake the heavens and earth during the final judgment. From the Exodus, Haggai uses imagery of chariots and their riders being overthrown (Exodus 14:28). He follows with the image of men in an army turning against one another as the Midianites did when fighting Gideon (Judges 7:21–22). Both of these are scenes in Israel's history where God fought for them. God is promising that he will again fight for his people.

But through whom will he do this blessing? Through whom will he fight? Remember that Israel had been promised over and over that the true king, the savior of Israel would come through the line of David. At this point, though Zerubbabel was the current governor, he was serving under the authority of Persia. Also, the Lord had spoken 130 years earlier of his rejection of Coniah through another prophet, Jeremiah, saying, "As I live, declares the LORD, though

Coniah the son of Jehoiakim, king of Judah, were the signet ring on my right hand, yet I would tear you off" (Jeremiah 22:24).

Let's break down what this means. First, a signet ring was a sign of royal authority, so the tearing off of Coniah as a signet ring meant the rejection of Coniah as king. Second, Coniah is better known as Jeconiah, grandfather of Zerubbabel, the governor of Judah. Third, not only had that king been rejected, but all of David's descendants had been rejected as king with him. God said through the prophet Jeremiah, "...for none of his offspring shall succeed in sitting on the throne of David and ruling again in Judah" (Jeremiah 22:30). If God had rejected David's line, and that line was to be the source of a savior, Israel could not be saved.

All of the above is why verse 23 contained words of great hope for Israel. The Lord of Hosts, meaning the commander of angel armies, declared that Zerubbabel—grandson of Coniah, member of the Davidic line that God had rejected so many years before—was being restored as God's servant. Zerubbabel would be given authority and would be used by God like a signet ring. As the king sealed a legal document with his signet ring, pressing the unique image in the ring into the soft wax that sealed a letter, so he would use a descendant of David. God's promise to bless his people through the line of David still stood.

But this promise was much bigger than Zerubbabel. If we fast forward about five hundred years to the genealogy of Jesus given in the third chapter of Luke, we find these names right in the middle: "the son of Joanan, the son of Rhesa, the son of Zerubbabel, the son of Shealtiel, the son of Neri" (Luke 3:27). God would indeed bless his people as they built his temple. Their "foundation day" anticipated God's dwelling with them once again. But this mighty God had plans to bless his people with his presence in a much, much greater way. In Jesus, the fullness of God came and dwelt among his people as he lived and walked around Judea for thirty-three years.

God continues to call his people to serve him, to give, and to build his temple, the church, where Jesus dwells by his Spirit. He waits to bless, to shower us with his encouragement if we will only put him first, hear his call to make disciples, and obey. As Joyce Baldwin writes, "He is waiting to bless, but He cannot do so while His people are apathetic and self-centered....Haggai's remedy for today, as for his own day, is a church mobilized for action, to which he would say, 'Take courage, work, fear not.'"[1]

Reflection Questions

4. On the day the people finished the foundation of the temple, they were both sobered by their sin and also joyful about their future, holding two conflicting emotions at once. Why is it important as Christians to make space both for being aware of our sin and for being joyful about what the Lord will do?

5. The unfinished work of the temple was making the people of God unclean. It showed their apathy and lack of interest in the things of God. Where currently in your life are you seeing your apathy toward the things of God show up?

6. God used the Israelites' circumstances to expose their hearts and turn them toward repentance. While not all difficulties are a rebuke or discipline from the Lord, he often uses circumstances to expose our hearts or change our course. When have you found this to be true for you?

7. While it is not a math equation that if we do "x" we get "y" from God, it is true that putting the kingdom first does lead to blessing and joy for the believer. What about this is comforting to you? What about this is confusing?

8. Prophesying through Haggai, the Lord gave the people the best news: God renewed his promise to send a messiah through the line of David, blessing his people with his presence in a deeper and fuller way. How do you think this news felt to them? How does it feel to you?

Focus verse

Is the seed yet in the barn? Indeed, the vine, the fig tree, the pomegranate, and the olive tree have yielded nothing. But from this day on I will bless you.

Haggai 2:19

Reflections, curiosities, frustrations:

Beyond the Border of Israel

The Book of Haggai ended with hope. God would keep his promise to give Israel a savior through the line of David. His people, who for years had struggled to have enough food, would be blessed and would see their fields and vines yield more than enough for themselves and their little ones.

Those promises were spoken through the prophet Haggai around 520 B.C. Fast forward a few decades to somewhere between 440 and 400 B.C. to again find God speaking to the people of Judah. Though some time had passed, the same temple still sat in Jerusalem. The same law of God was to be used by the Jews as they worshiped there. The same commitment to love and obey God's covenant was expected of God's people. Would the Jewish people honor God in the temple they had completed under the leadership of Zerubbabel and Joshua? Would they keep God's house as their priority over their own comfort?

It had been over fifty years since the temple was completed. Zerubbabel and Joshua—the men God had used to lead the people of Judah to finish the work—were dead. Though the final wood and stone had been put in place by around 516 B.C., God had still not come and visibly shown his glorious presence, filling the temple with himself as he had Solomon's temple hundreds of years before. Priests were making sacrifices and the daily ritual of the Lord's house continued, but the people's hearts were not committed to God. If anything, they doubted whether God was still committed to them.

Before we point fingers at the people of Judah (sometimes called Israel), let us consider their circumstances. Though dating the book of Malachi is difficult, most scholars estimate its writing to be around 460 B.C. Let that date sink in. This was the last book written before a silence of centuries with no prophet. After Malachi's ministry, it would be four hundred years until the next prophet, John the Baptist, came to prepare the way for Christ, who came in the flesh to save his people.

The city of Jerusalem was largely still in ruins with broken down walls. The people were still ruled by a foreign power, the Persians. The messiah who had been promised to come through the line of David (2 Samuel 7:12, Isaiah 11:1, Jeremiah 23:5–6) and who then was spoken of by Haggai (Haggai 2:22–23) had not yet come. The covenant promises given to Abraham (Genesis 15)—being a blessing to the world, being granted land of their own, and being as numerous as the stars—must have looked ridiculous in their current situation.

To top it off, the Edomites, Israel's favorite tribe to hate, were pushing into the territory where Israel currently lived. The Edomites were descendants of Esau, whose feud with Israel went back to Genesis 25. Abraham, the father of all Israel and the one to whom God first promised so many blessings for the world, had a son named Isaac. Isaac married Rebekah, who became pregnant with twins who fought in her womb before they were even born. They named the boys Jacob and Esau. Jacob's children, grandchildren, great-grandchildren, and so on eventually became the whole nation of Israel. Israel was chosen by God, for his own pleasure, by no merit of their own, to be his beloved and cherished people.

Esau's descendants, the Edomites, had a very different path. Instead of aligning themselves with the people of God, the Israelites, they mocked them in their pain. When the Babylonians were destroying Jerusalem and Israel was starving and hopeless, Edom gloated, stood aloof, and helped Israel's enemy. Obadiah 1:10–14 records God's rebuke of Edom for their mistreatment of Jacob's line. Soon after Jerusalem's destruction, the Edomites moved in and took over parts of the land.

The people of God were discouraged. They weren't sure God cared about them, so their lives began to reflect the fact that they didn't care about him either. Divorce was on the rise, tithing was neglected, and worship was a burden instead of a joy. When God's people experienced difficult days and didn't see God's promises fulfilled in their time, their faith wavered. They became apathetic and mistreated God and each other.

We, the twenty-first-century church, may also become discouraged in our difficult circumstances, whether individual or collective. We know God has promised beautiful redemption and the restoration of all things. But in our long waiting, whether for healing in this life or the one to come, we can begin to doubt God's love for us just as Israel did. Malachi reminds us as he did Israel that God always keeps his promises. In the meantime, we must live by faith and continue to obey

Re-read Malachi 1:1-5

Observation Questions

1. What does the Lord say in Malachi 1:2–3 about his relationship with Jacob versus his relationship with Esau?

2. Malachi 1:4, what does Edom say they will do? What does the Lord say he will do in response?

3. According to Malachi 1:5, what will Israel see and say?

Interpretation

Malachi 1:1–2. An "oracle" is literally a "burden" placed on a prophet by God himself. God had much to say to his people, and all of it came from his heart of love. He knew they were discouraged, so he began by reminding them of his affection for them. "I love you!" he told them. From there, Malachi began using a dialogue format to capture Israel's overall attitude toward God as if they were one person having a conversation with him. In this conversation, God would say something, a hypothetical response would be given, and God would answer. This dialogue may have even included the words of hecklers Malachi encountered in his public ministry. The book of Malachi consists of six of these dialogues (Malachi 1:2–5, 1:6–2:9, 2:10–16, 2:17–3:5, 3:6–12, 3:13–21) and a concluding summary (Malachi 4).

Warning: Malachi 1:2–3 may sound harsh to our modern ears. Keep in mind that these verses are not here primarily to make a statement about God's feelings or who he decides to help or align himself with. Rather, think about why God may have said these words to these people at this time. Imagine: you are an often-oppressed, small, weak nation that was mocked in your most terrible hour by a specific nation. To show his love for you, God is promising to punish those who were cruel to you when you needed their help. He pledges his allegiance to you and punishment and harsh treatment for them. It is as if God is saying, "I have your back. I am going to defend and stand up for you." After years of being in exile and returning to and living in devastation, this was probably a huge comfort to them. This is the context for Malachi 1:2–3.

In this verse, and especially when speaking of Jacob and Esau, love is not just a feeling or a passing warmth in the heart of God. God's love includes knowledge and action. It has consequences and traceable effects in Israel's history. When Israel (descendants of Jacob) responds to God's declaration of love with "How have you loved us?" God does not speak of his heart of affection or write them a love poem. He describes alliances and sovereign choice. He gives evidence of his work against their enemy and promises to continue punishing Edom. God's love is a powerful force when given to a person or group of people.

"How have you loved us?" Israel looked around their desolate city, the encroachment of Edom on their land, and the absence of God's visible glory in the temple and decided God didn't love them anymore. God's answer began with Jacob and Esau, using them as evidence of his sovereign choice of one and not the other. All Israelites would have known the story of Jacob and Esau, including their fight in Rebekah's womb before birth (Genesis 25:19–34). In effect, God was explaining to Israel that though these two men came from the same womb and could not have done anything before birth to make themselves more or less lovable, God chose to love one—Jacob—unconditionally.

God chose to protect, fight for, and bless Jacob's descendants for no other reason than God's own loving character. He loved them because he loved them. Because his love wasn't earned, his love didn't change. Deuteronomy 7:6b–8 speaks of this love:

> The LORD your God has chosen you to be a people for his treasured possession, out of all the peoples who are on the face of the earth. It was not because you were more in number than any other people that the LORD set his love on you and chose you, for you were the fewest of all peoples, but it is because the LORD loves you and is keeping the oath that he swore to your fathers, that the LORD has brought you out with a mighty hand and redeemed you from the house of slavery, from the hand of Pharaoh king of Egypt.

This is the same love and blessing he set upon Abraham and then Isaac. God would demonstrate his love for Isaac's son Jacob through his dealings with Jacob's enemy.

Malachi 1:3. God chose to use his power to bless and protect Jacob, in order to bless the entire world through his people. On the other hand, God set himself in opposition to Esau. Remember "love" and "hate" are not descriptions of feelings toward the individuals Jacob and Esau but, rather, declarations of God's choice to bless Jacob, though he did not deserve a blessing, and to work against Esau. This language of "love" and "hate" was often used in this time period when describing diplomatic relations between nations.

Jesus also used the language of "love" and "hate." Again, these words are not referring to emotions but rather to alignment and allegiance. He says in Luke 14:26: "If anyone comes to me and does not hate his own father and mother and wife and children and brothers and sisters, yes, and even his own life, he cannot be my disciple." Jesus was not calling people to act hatefully toward or reject anyone; rather, he was talking about aligning ourselves with his kingdom. Our allegiance and first loyalty must be with him.

By God's power he "laid waste" to, or made desolate, part of Edom's (Esau's descendants') land. The hills of Edom symbolized strength and security. But God had wilted and shriveled everything on those hills. Instead of a flourishing land full of bounty and livestock, the land of Edom was full of scavengers like jackals.

Though it may read to us like a cruel statement about Edom, this is actually a book of faithfulness toward Israel. In their depressed and discouraged state, God was telling his people, "I haven't forgotten about you. I still love you like I always have. Do you see what I've already done to your enemy's land? I remember what they did to you when the Babylonians destroyed Jerusalem, how they stood there and didn't help, how they mocked you. I will punish them for their cruelty to you." Other prophets record similar punishments of nations who were cruel to Israel or mistreated others. God demonstrates his sovereignty and encourages his people by dealing with their enemies.

Malachi 1:4–5. God's encouragement to his disheartened people continued. It seemed that while Israel was struggling economically, Edom was increasing in wealth and power. God promised that he would frustrate whatever recovery Edom made. Whatever they managed to build, he would tear down. And not only that, he would expose their sin in such a way that other nations would know they were wicked and that God was angry with them. God did not set his love on Jacob's descendants, Israel, because they were more inherently righteous than Esau's descendants. Israel deserved punishment for their many sins; the Old

Testament story is chock full of the shortcomings of Israel. God did discipline his people at times. But in loving Israel, God chose to show them his mercy. All of the nations had done things offensive to God, but he chose to love, align himself with, protect, and promote Israel—for no other reason than he chose to.

Is this not the gospel? We, the church, have experienced God's love in this way. All humans have sinned and fall short of the glory of God. But in his mercy he chose to love us. And in Christ he loves, aligns himself with, protects, and promotes us, showing us mercy we do not deserve.

God tells Israel that they will see what he does to Edom. In response, Israel will be wowed and in awe of the fact that God doesn't only work within their walls and their people; he is able and willing to show his glory and power to all nations. This fabulous display of God's character and ability will take their eyes off their own circumstances and draw them to the glory and capability of their God in the wider world.

God no longer has one chosen nation. He works by his Spirit among all nations to build for himself one church, united in Christ. And that church has enemies, just as Israel did. While the church's assailants may sometimes seem to have the upper hand, God will one day execute justice upon the church's enemies just as he did upon Edom and others. In the meantime, he reminds us of his promises in his Word, and calls us to live for the kingdom while we wait.

Reflection Questions

4. What did you learn about Israel's view on the Edomites? Do you think the modern-day church relates to any particular group in the same way?

5. Israel felt discouraged and unloved by God in Malachi's day, leading them to mistreat God and each other. When have you seen those two things linked: feeling God doesn't love you resulting in behaving in a way that mistreats God?

6. God's "hatred" of Edom is more accurately defined as rejection of Edom in contrast to his allegiance and acceptance of Israel. What is your response to God's choice in this?

7. God set his blessing on Jacob and his line that grew into Israel for no other reason than he chose to show them mercy because he loved them. Have you viewed God's love through Christ as something that has been set upon you or something that you obtained another way? Explain.

8. Through his actions toward Israel's enemy, God was showing the love and care he had for his people stretched beyond the "border of Israel" by God impacting parts of the world beyond them. When have you seen him impact something worlds away from your life but it was still encouraging to you?

Focus verse

Your own eyes shall see this, and you shall say, "Great is the Lord beyond the border of Israel!"

Malachi 1:5

Reflections, curiosities, frustrations:

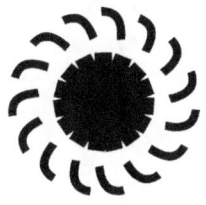

Study 5

Where Is My Honor?

Read Malachi 1:6–14

Observation Questions

1. In Malachi 1:6–8, what was Israel doing that was upsetting God?

2. According to Malachi 1:9–11, what did God want from his people?

3. List the things in Malachi 1:12–14 that the Lord says were profaning his name?

Interpretation

Worship at God's temple was never really about the animals. Everything in the Levitical law, the rules about animals, their condition, how to sacrifice them, and all the other statutes always pointed to and were meant for something greater—the relationship between God and his people. And yet, for a time, God chose to use the structure of animal sacrifice to provide a means of atonement for sin. Malachi called out the priests and their failure to properly handle the sacrifices given to God by his people.

Malachi 1:6a. The relationship between a father and son in the ancient Near East always followed a pattern. Honor was given to the father as a way to acknowledge his importance, his "weight," and his authority in the family. All of Malachi's listeners would have implicitly understood this. He took this pattern of relating and applied it to God and his people. After all, God had always related to his people as a father. Exodus 4:22 reads, "Then you shall say to Pharaoh, 'Thus says the LORD, Israel is my firstborn son…'" And yet, the priests of Israel were not honoring God as sons would have honored their fathers. They were not giving God the weight his glory deserved.

The relationship between a servant and master was another that all Israel would have understood. The master was in charge and was to be obeyed and feared by his servant. Yet again, Israel was neither obeying nor fearing their master, the

Lord. Not only were the priests not obeying; they were actually despising God's name in their work.

"Name" here is not just a proper noun used to point to God as we would point to a person. The name of God throughout the Bible means something much more. The greatness of God and the entirety of his character cannot be fully captured or comprehended by the human mind. And yet he chooses to reveal himself in order that we might have some small appreciation for the fullness of who he is. God's "name" is not just what we call him; it is his essence, his authentic being. It is all he is and all he does. To despise God's name was to despise God.

Malachi 1:6b–8. Malachi gave voice to the attitude of the priests of his day when he argued back, "How have we despised your name?" God's answer through Malachi: "By offering polluted food upon my altar." The word translated "polluted" does not mean "contaminated" but "unqualified" or "inappropriate." Still the priests did not understand. "How have we polluted you?" they asked. "By saying that the Lord's table may be despised." The priests had not uttered these words out loud, but their actions told everyone watching that it was ok to bring unfit sacrifices to God's table and therefore treat him with contempt.

Verse 8 finally describes some of the priests' offensive actions. They were offering blind, lame, and sick animals to God. These men whose job it was to instruct Israel in the proper worship and adoration of their God were instead defiling the very place where they had the privilege of serving him. This was not a mistake born out of ignorance. The priests knew the law, and they knew that no animal that was blind, disabled, or mutilated could be used as a food offering (Leviticus 22:22). They knew the same was true for the lame or blemished animals. And yet, they stood before the God of Israel day after day cutting up animals he expressly rejected.

Why would they do such a thing? We must remember that Israel was an agrarian group of people. Livestock was their livelihood, and giving up a healthy sheep was like handing over a large chunk of a bank account. Blind, lame, or blemished animals were worth less money and were worthless for breeding purposes. When the people brought these animals to the priests, it could have been viewed as advantageous for both parties. Many offerings called for meat to be cooked and shared as food between priests and Israelites. When the people brought a larger volume of sick, lame, or blind animals, both they and the priests got bigger meals. After all, blind lambs tasted the same as seeing lambs. Diseased animals could be used as burnt offerings, and no one would have to eat them at all. A cheap animal plus a bribe put more food on the priest's table than a whole animal plus obedience did.

The priests, whom Malachi was addressing here, had completely missed the point of the whole exercise of making sacrifices. God wanted their best, not their leftovers. He demanded the people's first fruits from the vine and field and first born from their herds. God had given Israel a picture of mercy and atonement, a way to understand how their sin was forgiven and to access God without being destroyed. The priests were making a mockery of God, treating him as if the ritual of killing animals were the point of the temple, rather than God meeting with his people.

In a moment of sarcasm, Malachi says to the priests, "Give those sick animals to your governor." Then he goes on to ask, "Will he accept them?" Of course he wouldn't. Not even a human authority would accept such animals as a gift. Even now we would never give someone we love or respect a defective gift. How much more should we refrain from giving the Lord himself something damaged.

Malachi 1:9–10. Malachi continued with a similar line of questioning: "Now intercede for us. After that kind of a gift, will God show you favor?" Again, the answer was, "Of course not!" God would not hear the priests as they offered him maimed, sick animals. Instead of honoring God as their authority, the priests were trying to appease him with mediocre and insulting sacrifices.

God would rather have someone shut the doors of the temple than continue to have the priests offer offensive sacrifices in his house. He was clear in verse 10 when he said, "I have no pleasure in you," meaning the priests. Ritualistic temple sacrifice with no devotion, honor, or love was worthless. It meant nothing to God.

Malachi 1:11. Despite how the priests were treating God and his reputation, the truth was that God was great, universally. He was reigning in power over all people, even as the priests were handling his house with such contempt. However, this verse was describing not just the present but also the future. It has an eschatological, or end-time, meaning. The present greatness of God and his reputation among the nations was only a foretaste of his future greatness. All nations—not just some—will eventually come to know God's greatness in its fullness. And all nations will see his greatness as it is, not as it was badly reflected by his disobedient chosen people.

The failure of the priests to properly lead the people in the sacrificial system would one day be remedied completely by a "pure offering," devoid of sin, blemish, or blindness—a perfect sacrifice would be given that would completely satisfy the debt humanity owed to God. The Messiah would offer himself as a sacrifice without the blemish or blindness of sin. The priests, who should have known God's real identity, failed to recognize his weightiness and honor and failed to show it to the world. But God himself would make his glory known, not only to Israel at the temple, but to all nations everywhere.

Though the people of Jerusalem would not see the fullness of this word in their day, the revealing of God's true power and authority had already begun to happen. We live in the already–not yet of the kingdom, where Christ has triumphed over death by his resurrection and ascension to the right hand of God. We are living in the end times, the last days. Though we do not yet see the total fullness of his glory, we have seen his beauty in Christ.

Malachi 1:12–13. What were the priests profaning or abusing by their actions? The Lord's name, his reputation, his character. The priests were annoyed and bored with their job as representatives of God to the people and of the people to God. They "snorted" or "turned up their nose" at God, bothered by the need to continue going through the motions of killing and offering animals to a God they didn't care about, and whom they didn't think cared about them.

Along with offering the sick and blind animals, the priests were offering God animals that had been mauled by other animals. These were not even to be eaten by humans, let alone given to a holy God (Exodus 22:31). Sacrificing in this way showed misunderstanding of the sacrificial system and all that it was pointing to, the perfect lamb of God. Sacrifices were futile when they were not accompanied by repentance, by faith, and by affection for and trust in God. Imagine if God offered a sinful man instead of Christ, the perfect God-man, on the cross. A sinful sacrifice on the cross would have accomplished nothing.

Because of the perfect sacrifice of Christ—the one to whom the entire sacrificial system pointed—we no longer worship at a temple or are required to bring animals to God. However, we now bring him the sacrifice of our praise and our lives. Hebrews 13:15–16 reads, "Through him then let us continually offer up a sacrifice of praise to God, that is, the fruit of lips that acknowledge his name. Do not neglect to do good and to share what you have, for such sacrifices are pleasing to God." The ritual of a church service and the acts of doing good and sharing what you have must also be accompanied by a heart of repentance, affection for the Lord, and faith in him. He does not need our worship, actions, or goods any more than he needed the sheep offered by the Israelites. However, we need his forgiveness, his presence, his help, his encouragement, and his love. Worship is a means of grace, a place where we can experience all of the above, have his truth spoken over us, and express our thanks to him.

Malachi 1:14. Not all sacrifices explained in the Old Testament law were mandatory. Voluntary thanksgiving offerings could be promised to God by a vow and then offered later at the altar. Sometimes these vows were made by Israelites when they were in a moment of suffering, danger, or duress, with a request that God would deliver them. This is the situation in view here. People were making such vows to worship God in a certain way but then bringing blemished animals after God had helped them. God declared such a person who did this "cursed." They had essentially lied to God.

We who lead God's people now also bear a special responsibility for the wellbeing of his people and for worship. God still has a certain structure and desire for worship, though it looks different than it used to. His Word instructs us to worship in spirit and in truth and offers many other directions for our public worship gatherings.

Up until now Malachi had been speaking to the priests about their malpractice. Here through Malachi God addressed the people as well: "For I am a great King, says the LORD of hosts." While we may picture a king who holds a mostly ceremonial role when we read this phrase, the ancient Near Easterner would have heard much more. A great king to them would have meant one that ruled other kings, the chief to whom all must bow. The Israelite priests should have known the greatness of the king whose offerings they were fooling with. One day, all would know. And yet the priests were bored and annoyed with the service of the King.

The perfect sacrifice that we could never offer came and offered himself in our place. He gave his unblemished, perfect life as a substitute for ours. How can we then do anything less than offer him back our whole selves, worshipping him in everything we do? As Paul wrote in Romans 12:1, "I appeal to you therefore, brothers, by the mercies of God, to present your bodies as a living sacrifice, holy and acceptable to God, which is your spiritual worship."

Reflection Questions

4. God, because of who he is, deserved honor and respect, but instead the Israelites' behavior showed that they despised him. When have you despised God? What circumstance led to that?

5. The people went through the motions of sacrificing animals for their sin, but they did it in a way that showed they really didn't care about the Lord, respect him, or feel connected to him. Do you see this type of heart attitude in the church? In your own life?

6. God's people were bored and turned up their nose at worship, not caring about God because they thought he didn't care about them. When have you been bored with worshiping God? What was the root cause of that for you?

7. Misuse of the sacrificial system didn't change the fact that it was pointing to the greatest sacrifice of all that was coming—Jesus himself. What does this tell us about God's love for his disobedient children both then and now?

8. God wants our hearts in worship, not just us going through the motions. What do you need to ask the Holy Spirit to help you with in this area?

Focus verse

For from the rising of the sun to its setting my name will be great among the nations, and in every place incense will be offered to my name, and a pure offering. For my name will be great among the nations, says the LORD of hosts.

Malachi 1:11

Reflections, curiosities, frustrations:

Study 6

Faithless

Read Malachi 2:1–16

Observation Questions

1. According to Malachi 2:5–8, what was the covenant that God made with the priests? In verses 8–9, what did the priests do in response?

2. According to Malachi 2:10–11, what had Judah done against God?

3. In Malachi 2:13–16, why was the Lord no longer regarding the people's offerings?

Interpretation

If we are ever tempted to be careless in our handling of God's Word for the good of his people, this passage should wake us up. God is totally committed to loving and caring for his people well. He would not allow the priests to continue leading Israel into dangerous sin by their lax example and blatant disobedience. He cares as deeply for his people now as he did then. We who lead in his church in any way must ask the Spirit to enable us to care well for his church.

Malachi 2:1–2. Chapter 1 ended with a word for all the people. Here Malachi again turned to the priests and rebuked them for their actions. In order to understand what was being cursed, we first must understand how the priests were blessed and how they were blessing others. Priests had a special standing in the nation of Israel. Part of the blessing they received was their closeness to God and their participation in sacred activities. They didn't have land of their own to grow crops and raise animals. Instead of the agrarian life of the rest of Israel, the priests worked in the temple, offering sacrifices for themselves and others. To provide for them, God required that all Israel bring a tenth, or a tithe, of their wealth to the temple. This provided for both upkeep on the temple and a salary for the priests.

Priests were also allowed to eat a portion of sacrifices brought by the people. They were to receive part of the grain offering (Leviticus 2:3), the baked grain offering (Leviticus 2:10), the sin offering (Leviticus 6:24–26), and the peace offering (Leviticus 7:31–32).

But priests, along with being blessed by their position, blessed others. The priests were to bless individual Israelites and their families with these words: "The LORD bless you and keep you; the LORD make his face to shine upon you and be gracious to you; the LORD lift up his countenance upon you and give you peace" (Numbers 6:24–26). The priests did not have a magic power that enabled them to distribute blessings to anyone they wanted. What they gave to the people was a reflection of God's attitude toward the people. If the people were acting in ways that went against the covenant, the covenant curses would come into effect.

Malachi 2:3. The curses continued. First, God said he would "rebuke" or "cut off" their descendants. Though families were important to all Israelites, the priests were especially affected by these words. The priesthood was familial, hereditary. To be a priest, one had to be born to the tribe of Levi (be a descendant of the man named Levi, one of Jacob's twelve sons) and in particular a son of Aaron's branch of the family. If there were no more sons, there was no more priesthood.

Was God really saying he would spread excrement on the faces of the priests? He was saying exactly that. Because of their work in the temple and the holiness of God, the priests were to be the most ceremonially clean people in the whole nation. There was an entire group of laws in the Old Testament devoted to their cleanliness; it included things like not touching dead human bodies, not eating certain foods, and not having sex for a certain number of days (Exodus 19:15, Leviticus 15). God was going to reverse their cleanliness and make them the most unclean, the least fit to be in his holy presence.

The excrement and innards of the animals that were sacrificed at the temple were to be taken out of the sanctuary before coming to the altar and burned on a heap. While the priests were used to pronouncing the shining of God's face upon his people, here God himself would smear the priests' faces with waste and leave them on the dung heap, the ultimate humiliation. God was serious about these men lovingly and carefully instructing his people in the way of the law. God had put them in a place to explain God's ways, including his forgiveness, to Israel. Their abuse of their office was a cruel twisting of God's loving word for his people. God would not let the priests continue to lead his people away from him.

Malachi 2:4–7. The purpose of God's rebuke to the priests was restoration. His words gave them the opportunity to stop making a mockery of the temple and start worshipping the way he had asked them to. What was the covenant of Levi to which he refers? No biblical passage records it explicitly, but two passages refer to some sort of covenant made with the sons of Aaron, Levitical priests: Numbers 25:10–13 and Jeremiah 33:21. Broadly speaking it probably referred to all responsibilities given to the priests by the Old Testament law. God was rebuking in order to restore.

The covenant God had given Levi included "life," referring to long life and a perpetual priesthood. It also included "peace"—shalom—which involves care, preference, protection, and wholeness. All of these things were given by God for the priests who "feared," or held a deep reverence for, him and worked that reverence out in their obedience to him, performing their jobs in accordance with the law. Those Levitical priests taught the people faithfully and also lived with integrity. Their good influence led many others to obey God. All of this led to the prospering and flourishing of his people, the shalom God wished for them.

As verse 7 pointed out, priests were supposed to take their knowledge of the law together with their years of life lived in integrity and act as individual counselors to Israelites who needed direction in certain situations. They were to show God's people how to live God's way, in order that they might know his goodness and his blessing.

Malachi 2:8–9. The priests of Malachi's time failed to do any of the above. Instead of guarding the law, they ignored what was written in it, taking bribes and sickly animals. Their bad example led many to follow it and also disregard God's law in their worship practices. Instead of turning people away from their sin and acting as examples of righteousness, they showed people new ways to sin.

What does it mean to corrupt a covenant? First, a word here about covenants in the ancient Near East: A covenant was an agreement between two parties. The most common type was that of a suzerain-vassal covenant. This was a treaty made between a more powerful and a less powerful entity or person, usually between a king and a group of people. The more powerful person or group issued the terms and also enforced them. The powerful suzerain offered benefits like protection from enemies and land, while the less powerful vassal promised tribute and loyalty to the suzerain. These covenants came with blessings and curses, the consequences of the vassal either keeping the terms or breaking the terms.

The covenant of Levi was this type of agreement. If the priests, the descendants of Levi— the lesser, or "vassals," in this agreement—continued to fail to keep the terms, they would incur the curses that had been promised by God. These curses were not a surprise or a new punishment God spontaneously thought up in his anger. The terms between parties had been agreed upon long before this generation of priests entered the world. When Malachi wrote in verse 9, "And so

I make you despised and abased before all people, inasmuch as you do not keep my ways…," this was simply a statement of the priests' breach of the contract. God saw their hypocrisy. He would reveal it so that all the people would see their hypocrisy as well.

God's words about ending the priesthood were not an empty threat. The priesthood did end soon after Malachi's ministry in that a greater high priest came and rendered the previous one obsolete. Not only that, the destruction of the temple in 70 A.D. meant there was no longer a place for a sacrificial system. The Romans finally kicked the Jews out of the city of Jerusalem altogether soon after the temple was destroyed.

It was not only these priests' failure that was bringing an end to the era of the Levitical priesthood. A better priest was coming, one who would never be corrupted by a bribe or lead anyone astray by his lazy example. The Messiah, Christ, would offer himself as a lamb without blemish in a once-for-all sacrifice for sin. He would love his people by clearly showing them God's forgiveness and the way to attain it. The writer of Hebrews spoke of Jesus as this priest in Hebrews 7:26–27, "For it was indeed fitting that we should have such a high priest, holy, innocent, unstained, separated from sinners, and exalted above the heavens. He has no need, like those high priests, to offer sacrifices daily, first for his own sins and then for those of the people, since he did this once for all when he offered up himself." Every requirement of the sacrificial law was fulfilled by Jesus's sacrifice.

Malachi 2:10–12. "We" here means fellow Jews. How had the Jews been faithless to one another and "profaned the covenant of our fathers"? The "covenant" was that of Sinai, which the people agreed to in Exodus 19. God agreed to be Israel's God and their rescuer. The people offered their loyalty and obedience to God's law. Part of that law included only marrying other Israelites. The purpose of this law was not to keep other ethnicities out of the nation of Israel—consider Rahab or Ruth, who were welcomed because of their faith in the God of Israel. Instead, it was to guard a true faith in Yahweh.

The Israelites had been "faithless to one another" or "betrayed one another" (another accurate translation) by marrying members of other faiths. When an Israelite man married "the daughter of a foreign god," he married a woman who worshiped a god other than Yahweh and would almost certainly compromise his own faith eventually.

The Israelites probably intermarried in order to be granted jobs by foreigners and to get better trade deals because of family ties. Also, foreign gods allowed women to be treated as sex objects while Israel's God did not. Malachi asked God to remove any Israelites who intermarried from his people, in order that idol worship among his nation would die out. Since it was this type of idol worship that led to the exile in the first place, attention had to be paid by Israel that the same sin didn't take hold again.

Malachi 2:13–14. How else were the Israelites betraying their covenant with God, or not keeping their agreement with him? Instead of offering sacrifices to thank him for his love, protection, and provision, they were trying to manipulate him with loud emotional displays at the temple. Foreign gods were said to be "moved" by these types of displays, including worshipers hurting themselves (remember the prophets of Baal in the showdown with Elijah in 1 Kings 18 and how they cut themselves). The God of Israel was not to be manipulated into action but obeyed in love.

Israelites were also copying their pagan neighbors by practicing something called "aversion divorce." Israelite men who had been promised to Israelite women by their parents, sometimes even before birth but definitely before puberty, got tired of their first wives, here called "the wife of your youth." Their first weddings included a covenant between the bride and groom, an agreement between equals. All covenants at that time had a witness who was to ensure that it was enforced. God was the witness in these young marriages and would stand up for the wives who had no advocate to help them. Though the law did not necessarily prohibit second marriages at this time, it would not allow for divorce from a first wife just because the husband was bored with her or no longer wanted to support her.

Malachi 2:15–16. Malachi wasn't done talking about divorce.[1] He was saying that just as God's people were bound by the fatherhood of their one God, so a married couple was bound by God's Spirit. God did this for the sake of the children that would be born to that couple and would therefore be under the same covenant, agreement, or promise. Verse 15 was telling Israelite men, "Be faithful to your first wife!" The one who divorces his wife "covers his garment with violence." Divorce left a public mark on the husband, both in God's eyes and in the eyes of the community. "You've got blood on your hands" would capture this phrase well.[2]

God made a covenant with his people through Moses at Sinai, beginning with these words: "I am the LORD your God, who brought you out of the land of Egypt, out of the house of slavery" (Exodus 20:2). God first rescued his people, then called them to obedience through his word. He promised to protect and provide, and asked for their loyalty. Unlike the unfaithful husbands of Israel, God is always faithful to his word and has kept his side of the agreement. Though the priests and people of Israel failed in their worship, the fact that he sent Malachi to speak to them is evidence that he had not abandoned them. God's love for them was persistent, as it is for us today when we are unfaithful.

The Lord had been nothing but faithful to his people. He cared for them, taught them, guided them, and provided for them, only to have his priests and people turn around and act unfaithfully both to him and each other. This faithless behavior of God's people reflected how far their hearts were from him. The faithful God was calling his people to reflect him with faithfulness themselves. Lord, may this be true of us, your church.

Reflection Questions

4. God had put the priests in place to lovingly care for his people and teach them the law, but instead they misused their position, dishonoring God and damaging God's people. When have you seen this happen in the church? What was the result?

5. In this text God makes it clear that he was not okay with priests misusing his word and hurting his people giving them strong consequences for that. What do you find comforting about that? What do you find confusing?

6. Judah was acting faithlessly to one another by marrying people of differing faiths, in hopes they would get some financial gain, instead of following what the Lord had instructed regarding marriage. What insight does this give you about God's people and marriage? Why do you think this is important?

7. God's people were acting faithlessly by divorcing their wives because they wanted new, younger wives, squandering the union that God had put a portion of his Spirit into. What new insight does this give you about marriage? About divorce?

8. God has always been faithful to his people. He wants his people to be faithful to him and to each other. Where are you struggling with faithfulness? What do you need to repent of and ask the Lord for help with?

Focus verse

Have we not all one Father? Has not one God created us? Why then are we faithless to one another, profaning the covenant of our fathers?

Malachi 2:10

Reflections, curiosities, frustrations:

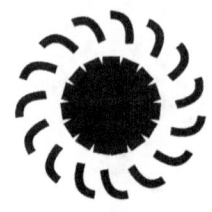

Study 7

The Lord Whom You Seek

Read Malachi 2:17–3:12

Observation Questions

1. In Malachi 2:17–3:2 what were the people of God doing or saying, and what was the Lord going to do in response?

2. What does Malachi 3:1–4 say the messenger will do when he comes? What will "the Lord whom you seek" do when he comes?

3. Summarize Malachi 3:6–12.

Interpretation

God continued to speak to his wayward priests and people through Malachi. But in these words of warning and rebuke is the promise of hope. An answer to the questions of the people was coming, and a messenger was coming first to prepare the way. The Lord himself would refine and purify his people so that they again pleased him.

Malachi 2:17. In this fourth dialogue between God and his people, Israel didn't understand how they had worn the Lord out. God answered by pointing out that they were saying things like: "Everyone who does evil is good in the sight of the Lord, and he delights in them." Or by asking, "Where is the God of justice?" Because of their hard experiences, Israel came to the conclusion that God loved evildoers. He was allowing the wicked to continue in their evil ways without punishment. "Where is the God of justice?" they asked. In their estimation, the God of justice they thought they had known was no longer around. The Israelites wanted justice from God for themselves, even though many of them were not doing justice to their hired workers, to widows, to the fatherless, or to sojourners (people temporarily residing outside their home country).

When the circumstances of our lives are difficult, we, too, may begin to wonder if God is different than what we thought. We may look at our neighbors or coworkers who seem to live only for themselves and against God's kingdom and ways, wondering why God seems to allow them to go on without consequence. They get richer, stay healthy, get promoted, and live what looks like an easy life while we endure suffering. But God does not work on our timeline any more than he worked on that of the people to whom Malachi spoke. God will judge in his own time. Our current material circumstances are not the evidence of his love for or commitment to us.

Malachi 3:1–2. In answer to the people asking, "Where is the God of justice?" (Malachi 2:17), God reassured them that he was coming and that he would send a messenger before him. It was the practice of kings in the ancient Near East to send a messenger to the people he planned to visit. The messenger not only told the people of the king's upcoming visit but literally cleared the physical way for him to come, sometimes creating roads and cutting down trees. God promised to send someone like this ahead of himself. Luke recorded the life of this messenger sent before Jesus, John the Baptist, in Luke 3:1–22. John did prepare the way for Jesus's coming, but instead of preparing roads and bridges, John prepared hearts for the coming of the true King.

God was saying something magnificent in verse 1: "And the Lord whom you seek will suddenly come to his temple." God was promising to send his Son to personally visit the temple and bring the justice the people longed for. If the people were looking for God, they would certainly see him. He would suddenly and surprisingly appear. This can be nothing else but a reference to John the Baptist, the messenger, and Jesus, the Messiah.

The people expected that the coming of the God of justice would be a good thing for them. But God knew their hearts. His words "in whom you delight" are probably sarcastic. The people of Israel did not delight in his covenant with them at this point. They mocked it. Malachi gave a warning about the one coming to them in verse 2.

When the Messiah came, it would be difficult for anyone to stand their ground during his testing. He would come like a fire that purifies or a bleach that whitens, removing impurities from his people. He would come to separate those who adhered to his covenant from those who did not. His coming would be difficult and refining. His work would be good for his people but not pleasant.

We must note here that Malachi was not predicting judgement on the basis of works. God's covenant people were sinners just as we are and could never live a perfectly holy life without God's help. But he had given them the hope of his salvation if they would entrust themselves to his grace. They were to look to the temple and the sacrifices in faith for their forgiveness, giving him their loyalty and trust. That temple and those sacrifices pointed to Christ, the perfect sacrifice. Just as the Israelites looked forward to his salvation, so we look back at his life, death, and resurrection in faith.

Malachi 3:3–4. The Lord would not only be like the fire that purifies but would be the refiner himself. The picture here is that of a silversmith, patiently putting the silver through the fire until the dross had burned off. God would do this with his priests until they brought offerings to him in the way they were supposed to be offered. This would please him, both the offerings themselves and those bringing them. There had been eras in Israel's history where God had been pleased with the priest's offerings. Another pleasing era was coming. We as believers live in such an era, where Christ's offering totally satisfies the Lord, leaving him pleased with us who put our faith in his sacrifice.

Malachi 3:5. Just as some would be purified in order to please God when he came, so some would be judged. All those listed in this verse were breaking God's law. Those who "oppress the hired worker in his wages" either promised one wage and then gave less or didn't pay the worker their wages immediately at the end of the day. These workers lived hand-to-mouth and couldn't survive if they weren't paid every day. Widows, orphans, and sojourners had no protectors or advocates. God would be a witness against those who mistreated these defenseless people and obviously did not fear God. Again, this is still God's answer to the people's question, "Where is the God of justice?" God was answering, "I am coming. And you will see my justice. Which side will you be on when I come?"

Malachi 3:6–7. To the people's complaint that God had changed and now loved people who did evil, God said this: "I, the LORD, do not change." The only reason Israel still existed was because God had not changed. His faithfulness and grace were the same as they had always been.

But Israel had not changed, either! They had been unfaithful as they murmured against Moses in the desert, unfaithful when they asked for a king so they could be like all the other nations, and they were still unfaithful. As always, God offered them a chance to repent, change their ways, and come back to him. He told them, "Return to me, and I will return to you." The people, in their ignorance, backsliding, apathy, and discouragement, did not know how to return to God.

Had God left his people? Yes, in the sense that he was not blessing them as he would have been if they had been obediently loving and trusting him, treating him and his temple as he asked. God had promised this consequence in Deuteronomy 31:16b–17 when he said, "they will forsake me and break my covenant that I have made with them. Then my anger will be kindled against them in that day, and I will forsake them and hide my face from them, and they will be devoured. And many evils and troubles will come upon them, so that they will say in that day, 'Have not these evils come upon us because our God is not among us?'"

However, even if God was not blessing his people, his presence was still everywhere. His common grace was still given to the whole world, bringing rain and sunshine, causing their hearts to beat, and sustaining their little ones. Because of

God's grace, judgement was not the end of their story but a way to discipline them. Even though he had turned his favor away from them, they were still his chosen people.

Malachi 3:8–9. Everything Israel had belonged to God. He had commanded them to give ten percent of everything they had to the temple. This provided food and money for the priests, as well as money for the upkeep of the temple. When the people didn't do this, they robbed his priests and therefore robbed God. The priests had to either accept bribes or leave their work at the temple to grow and raise their own food. Those who serve the church vocationally today still rely on God's people giving to God out of their wealth.

The "storehouse" was that of the temple. God was answering the people's question of how they might return to him. His answer was that they must test his goodness by bringing the full tithe to him. This was not necessarily a promise that if an individual man or family brought their ten percent to the temple, God would turn their financial situation around. But if all of Israel would turn and obey in this way, they would have all the food they needed and more. The "windows of heaven" that God would open were those of rain, which the people needed to quench the drought they were enduring. Remember that Israel was a people that lived off the land. Without rain, they could not eat. God would "pour down" the blessing of rain until they had exactly what they needed.

It still remains true that everything we have belongs to God. He still calls us to give a portion back to him. As Paul wrote in 2 Corinthians 9:6–8, "The point is this: whoever sows sparingly will also reap sparingly, and whoever sows bountifully will also reap bountifully. Each one must give as he has decided in his heart, not reluctantly or under compulsion, for God loves a cheerful giver. And God is able to make all grace abound to you, so that having all sufficiency in all things at all times, you may abound in every good work."

Malachi 3:11–12. Not only would God give the rain they needed, he would protect their crops from the devourer, the locust. Their work in the fields would bear fruit. In fact, their fields would bear so much that surrounding nations would take notice and call Israel blessed. Those who saw Israel would envy what they saw and wonder at such a generous God.

The messenger did come. Jesus came as a refiner, with John sent before him to prepare the way. Jesus came to purify his people, and he brought an offering of righteousness to the Lord (Malachi 3:3). God and his faithfulness still have not changed. We, like the Israelites are fickle and forgetful, apathetic and easily discouraged. But Jesus made a way for us to return to him by faith, over and over and over again.

Reflection Questions

4. The Israelites assumed God did not care about injustice when they saw unjust people receiving what felt like blessing. When have you felt the same way?

5. Malachi was predicting judgement because the people's hearts were not looking to the temple and sacrifices—which pointed to the true salvation coming for them in Christ—for forgiveness. How does this help you understand Old Testament people and how they either trusted or did not trust in the future hope of Christ?

6. The promise of the Messiah was spoken to these wayward, disobedient people in Malachi's time. What does this tell you about how far reaching God's salvation is for his people?

7. Malachi 3:5 lists things God will judge as injustice. Which part of this list surprises you? In which area on this list do you struggle to act justly?

8. Due to the disobedience and disrespect of his people, God removed his blessing from them. But he did not remove his common grace, which still impacted so much of their daily lives. What does this tell you about God and how he fathers us?

9. Tithing in this passage is less about an individual tithing resulting in blessing and more about God's people collectively showing trust in him by tithing. What new insight on tithing does this text give you?

Focus verse

Behold, I send my messenger, and he will prepare the way before me. And the LORD whom you seek will suddenly come to his temple; and the messenger of the covenant in whom you delight, behold, he is coming, says the LORD of hosts.

Malachi 3:1

Reflections, curiosities, frustrations:

Study 8

Treasured Possession

Read Malachi 3:13–4:6

Observation Questions

1. What things did God say the people had said against him in Malachi 3:13–15?

2. According to Malachi 3:16–18, what did those who feared the Lord do and what did the Lord say he would do in response?

3. According to Malachi 4:1–3, what will happen to the arrogant and all evildoers? What will happen to those who fear the Lord?

Interpretation

For any of us who have ever felt like walking in faithfulness to God seems futile, that it has done us no good, or that those who do not walk with God seem to live the good life with no consequences for their actions, this is a passage for our encouragement. God, in fact, does notice all of our actions, our sacrifices, and our attempts to please him. Those who live for themselves and not for him will be judged. And we who have suffered and struggled by faith, even weak faith, on the great day of the Lord will jump around like young calves, exuberant, full of joy, and completely satisfied. We must live now in light of that day.

Malachi 3:13–14. The people of Judah accused God of being unjust and pleased with wicked people. "Hard words," said the Lord. But the people didn't even see how cynical they'd become. The Lord reminded them of their true attitude. They had decided it wasn't worth serving God, that there was not even any reason to mourn before him. Mourning is what the people of God would have done had they believed God cared about them. They would have worn sackcloth, sat in the dust, and cried out to God in repentance or lament so that he might see their situation and help. Instead, they decided only to go through the motions of sacrifice while protecting their hearts from the God they thought had failed them.

Living by faith in God's promises seemed futile; it seemed to them that those who lived for themselves rather than God had better circumstances. So Israel chose flagrant disobedience of God's laws.

The "arrogant," those who ignored the covenant, were being called the lucky ones. Not only did those who did evil seem to do well financially; they also "put God to the test" by openly disobeying God's law with their attitude and actions. They mocked God with their lives—knowing full well he had called them to give their loyalty to him—and dared him to respond.

Malachi 3:16. Don't miss this: something very good is about to happen among a nation who has so far not responded to Malachi's preaching. Some of them actually heard his words and took them to heart, leading to real repentance. Not all of Judah but a group of those within it met together to talk about Malachi's words and their own sin. This group went against what the rest of Israel was saying. They disagreed with their brothers' and sisters' assessment of God that he was unjust and that he didn't hold evil people accountable.

These repentant brothers and sisters recorded their belief in the justice, goodness, and faithfulness of God on a scroll, signing their names as those turning from the cynicism, apathy, and mocking worship practices of their day. This document was one of renewal, encouragement, and faith. It was a testimony to their belief that God did, indeed, see and that he does notice the faith of those who love God and will punish those who do not.

Malachi 3:17–18. God has a declaration to make about those who, not perfectly but truly, love and fear him. The "mine" is emphasized in Hebrew. They will belong to him and him alone. Those who lived by faith in Israel would be God's "treasured possession." This little phrase was used by kings to describe their own private property, which was surrounded by everything else they ruled over in their kingdom. God would spare these treasured people from punishment, as a father spares his loved son. The remnant—those who endure by God's grace—is his treasured possession, the true Israel.

In verse 18, God says he will "once more" show his people that the righteous and the wicked will experience different things both in the present and in the future. The righteous will be found innocent and the wicked guilty. He had spoken this through the prophets for many years, but he would continue to do so. Both kinds of people could be found within Israel.

We must remember that it was not national affiliation or tradition that saved the Israelites. Circumcision of the body (required for all Israelite men as a sign of their membership in the covenant) without circumcision of the heart meant nothing. As Paul wrote in Romans 9:6, "For not all who are descended from Israel belong to Israel." The same is true today for those in the church. It is not church membership or Sunday morning attendance that saves a soul. Rather, those things are the fruit of the faith of those who have already been saved, who already know they are loved and treasured by God.

Malachi 4:1. When will God show the distinction between the one who serves and loves God and the one who doesn't? When will it be extremely obvious to all that those two groups of people have very different futures? On "the day," the day of the Lord, when he comes to judge, to acquit those who have been living by faith and punish those who have not. The day of the Lord here refers to the first coming of Christ into the world to initiate his kingdom. But it also refers to the time we're living in now, as the kingdom is growing but has not yet grown into its fullness, which will reach its culmination when Jesus returns to judge the earth. The prophets often talk about the coming of the Messiah as if it is a one-time event. The surprise of history is that Jesus's first coming inaugurated his kingdom. He returned to his father, and his kingdom is *still* growing. His return will bring the kingdom to its culmination.

That day will burn like an oven. It will burn so hot that those who do not fear the Lord will burn like a dried out field that catches fire and is charred down to the roots. There will be no escape. Those who were listed in Malachi 3:5—sorcerers; adulterers; those who swear falsely; those who oppress the hired worker in his wages, the widow, and the fatherless; those who thrust aside the sojourner; and those who do not fear the Lord—will be judged.

Malachi 4:2–3. What will happen to those who fear the Lord? To those who by the grace of God have remained loyal to him and his covenant? They will be protected from judgement and healed, not only from illness but also from their losses through all sorts of tragedy and trauma. This healing will include restoration, peace, and full life. It will include healing even from the damage caused by their own sin. By the wounds of his perfect sacrifice, the coming Messiah will heal all the wounds of his people.

Malachi's audience would have been familiar with multiple images of the sun with wings. The Persians worshipped a deity that was usually drawn with a winged sun disk. A king with this disk as his symbol was under the protection of that god. Egyptians, Sumerians, Assyrians, and Hittites all worshipped a sun god depicted by the same image. But Malachi knew true healing was found in the wings of the Lord, the one who actually makes the sun rise and set on all people. It is his warmth and protection that brings life. He co-opted this image, as other biblical authors often do with pagan or foreign images, and used it to represent the only true safety and vitality, given by the Lord.

The second half of Malachi 4:2 is one of the most joyful images from the entire Old Testament. On the day of the Lord when he comes to judge the earth, those who are found to be his, who belong to him, who have committed themselves to him by faith, will kick and buck and run like young calves. Young calves love to run and jump and playfully stomp their hooves on the ground as part of their muscle development. When these types of calves are let out of the stall, they almost look like they're dancing as they gleefully jump and buck. This is how those who belong to God will feel on that great day, full of joy, freed of all that bound them.

On that day as God's people jump like calves, they will be jumping on the ashes of the wicked. Malachi made this announcement to Israel that those who were holding desperately onto faith might be encouraged to continue and to live out their faith with right worship practices. We struggle through suffering and the mocking of our God by others who claim his name. But one day we will jump and rejoice, dancing on the ashes of God's enemies. Of course our hope is that the wicked would convert and join with God's people. But ultimately, God will deal with the wicked with his justice. His enemies will no longer be a problem for his people. In fact, they'll be like dust under their feet.

Malachi 4:4–6. And what should the covenant faithful do in the meantime? They should remember the law given to Moses at Horeb (another name for Sinai) and live by it. Faith does not exist for the sake of faith. Faith moves us to obey the one in whom we trust.

God's last word in Malachi serves as a sort of bridge between the Old and New Testaments, though Malachi could not have known that four hundred years would pass before another word would be heard from the Lord. The Lord would send someone before he came himself. "Elijah the prophet" in verse 5 is surely John the Baptist, the forerunner of Jesus. This man would turn the hearts of fathers and sons back to the Lord, and therefore back toward one another. This was a picture of general familial reconciliation, a symbol for the larger restoration and renewal that was coming for God's people.

"Utter destruction" in verse 6 was spoken of in other passages as final and irreversible judgement and destruction of evil persons (Deuteronomy 7:2, Joshua 10:39, 1 Samuel 15:3). "Elijah," referring to John the Baptist, is promised in order that this type of destruction might be avoided.

We believers live after the first coming of Christ, in the last days. We have not yet seen the complete fulfillment of Malachi's words. However, Christ's kingdom has come in part. He did offer himself as a perfect sacrifice. Because of his work, we no longer have to go to the temple and offer God animals and grains to find forgiveness of sin. There is no need for a temple where God can dwell, because Christ came and dwelled closely with his people. And now he dwells by his Spirit in the church, God's covenant people.

But, total fulfillment of Malachi's prophecy is coming. There will be a separation of those who mock God from those who obey God, of those who live by faith in their own accomplishments from those who live by faith in Christ's sacrifice. It may look now as if those who are against Christ have the good life and stroll through life without hindrance. But their destiny will be made known, as will ours. All the sacrifices for the sake of Christ, the money given, the angry words held in, the orphans patiently loved, the seeds sown in faith, the immigrants and refugees welcomed, the opportunities to cheat passed over, the countless prayers spoken, the service to the kingdom, all will be recognized.

"How have you loved us?" asked the people of Malachi's day in Malachi 1:2. God answered them by punishing their enemies, rebuking their priests for their own good, promising the blessing of rain on their crops, holding out the hope of another Elijah and then a messiah to follow, and giving them a vision of unfettered joy.

But God answered that question even more loudly hundreds of years later. He came in the flesh to seek and save the lost. He dwelled not just in the temple but among his people as he "tabernacled" among them (John 1:14). He died as the perfect sacrifice for our sins, was raised from the dead, and ascended to the right hand of the Father. He sent the Spirit to minister to us and indwells the church by the same. On the day when Jesus returns, we will not be able to count the ways that God has shown his love for us.

Reflection Questions

4. God's people struggled to live by faith in a time when they looked around and felt like God's promises seemed futile and ineffective. How can you relate to them?

5. Some of the people in response to Malachi's words repented and trusted in the Lord. When have you seen a group of believers repent? What was that like?

6. For those who follow and fear the Lord, even imperfectly, he calls us his "treasured possession." How does this impact your view of how God thinks of you?

7. When the Lord returns in the second coming, judgment and punishment will come for those who do not fear and trust the Lord. Malachi gives vivid descriptions of that. How often do you think about that? What is your response to this truth?

8. When the Lord returns in the second coming, freedom and joy will come for those who fear and trust the Lord. They will be free from all that harmed and bound them in this life—so much so that they will look like frolicking, free baby calves. How often do you think about that? What is your response to this truth?

9. Write down a few takeaways from studying the books of Haggai and Malachi.

Focus verse

They shall be mine, says the LORD of hosts, in the day when I make up my treasured possession, and I will spare them as a man spares his son who serves him. Then once more you shall see the distinction between the righteous and the wicked, between one who serves God and one who does not serve him.

Malachi 3:17–18

Reflections, curiosities, frustrations:

Acknowledgments

Hope: Writing these studies has changed my life in so many big and little ways. At least once a book Chris and I say, "Can you believe we get to do this?" Chris, I hope the Lord always lets us keep doing this! Thank you to all you sisters who buy our studies and share them with others. Thank you, Ray, for always cheering me on and reminding me of the main goal in all of this. Jen, thank you for being on the team in every sense of the word—we run so much better with you around. To my Friday morning sisters who did the pilot with me at one of the busiest times of the year, your presence made this study better and made me feel so supported!

Chris: Michael, you're the first and best At His Feet consultant, and my favorite. Hope, I'd pick you as my partner every time. Jen and Renae, you make the dream team dreamy, and I love you big. Dr. Goldstein, again you've been a fabulous team member; we're so thankful for you. Heather, Nadia, and Elizabeth, your encouragement means more than you know. Elliot, we believe in you, so we did what you said!

Notes and Further Reading

Study 1. This House Lies in Ruins: Haggai 1:1–11

1. J. Alec Motyer, "Haggai," in *The Minor Prophets, Volume 3: A Commentary on Zephaniah, Haggai, Zechariah, Malachi,* edited by Thomas Edward McComiskey (Grand Rapids, MI: Baker Academic, 1998), 974.

2. A note about translations: Translating from any one language to another is never a one-to-one process with perfect overlap; we always have to make interpretive choices. Different translations lean different ways. Some are more word for word and may read a bit clunkier than those that translate idea for idea, attempting to be more dynamic and closer to our speech patterns. For more on this, see chapter 2 of *How to Read the Bible for All Its Worth* by Gordon D. Fee and Douglas Stuart (Grand Rapids, MI: Zondervan Academic, 2014). Or, just look at the preface or introduction to your current Bible. Most include their philosophy of translation.

Study 2. Work, for I Am with You: Haggai 1:12–2:9

1. See Matthew 2:11, where the kings bring their wealth to the baby Messiah, and Revelation 21:24–26, where the glory of nations is brought into the city.

Study 3. I Have Chosen You: Haggai 2:10–23

1. Joyce Baldwin, *Haggai, Zechariah, Malachi: An Introduction and Commentary* (Downers Grove, IL: Intervarsity Press, 1972), 55.

Study 6. Faithless: Malachi 2:1–16

1. Some translations, such as the NKJV and NASB, have translated Malachi 2:16 to include the phrase "I hate divorce." While this is a difficult verse to translate, Dr. C. John Collins, Old Testament editor of the ESV Bible, makes a compelling argument that the subject of the verb "hate" (that is, the person doing the hating) is an Israelite who divorces his wife, not the Lord.

2. Douglas Stuart. "Malachi" in *The Minor Prophets, Volume 3,* 1,343.

Further Reading

Beth Glazier-McDonald, *Malachi: The Divine Messenger,* Society of Biblical Literature Dissertation Series 98 (Atlanta, GA: Scholars Press, 1987).

Philip J. King and Lawrence E. Stager, *Life in Biblical Israel* (Louisville, KY: Westminster John Knox Press, 2002).

Pieter A. Verhoef, *The Books of Haggai and Malachi,* Eerdmans Classic Biblical Commentaries (Grand Rapids, MI: Eerdmans, 1987).

The Story of At His Feet Studies

A few years ago, Hope started looking for materials for the women's fall Bible study at our church. While she found a great number of quality Bible studies, she had a hard time finding studies written for women by women who were reformed. She also had a tough time finding in-depth studies of the Scripture that didn't take a whole lot of time. In a moment of desperation, Hope asked Chris if she would be willing to co-write a study on Romans, convincing her by asking, "I mean, really, how hard could it be?" And so it began. Weekly emails back and forth, Chris deep in commentaries, Hope mulling over questions, tweaking, editing, asking, pondering. A group of women at Redeemer Presbyterian Church in Lincoln, Nebraska, patiently bore with us as we experimented with them every week and learned to find our rhythm as writers.

Two years later, Hope approached Chris again, softening her up by telling her she could choose any book she wanted: 1 Samuel it was. Old Testament narrative is the best. Another study was born. About this time, women started asking us for copies of the two studies we had written. While trying to send endless PDFs to people around the country via email, a pastor friend who happens to be a publisher approached Chris and Hope at a party, offering to publish the Bible studies. Suddenly, we had a way to get these into the hands of women who could use them. This had been the point of the whole enterprise—to help make the book of Romans accessible to women. But what would the name be?

During the first century, when Jesus walked the earth, a Jewish rabbi would have been surrounded by his students, with some of the men sitting at his feet to learn and listen. This was the custom, the understood norm of the day. But in Luke 10:39, *Mary* sat at the feet of Jesus. Mary, a woman, was taught by this unconventional rabbi. Mary was given the dignity of taking in his words, his pauses, his tone. To Jesus, she was every bit as worthy of his teaching as the men in the room were—and so are we, his women students today. And so we are At His Feet Bible Studies, hoping to sit at the feet of Jesus while we study his Word.

Other At His Feet Studies

We pray that you will continue to sit at the feet of Jesus, studying his Word. To help you with this, we have also written these Bible studies:

1 Samuel (16 studies)
Psalms (13 studies)
Lamentations (7 studies)
Luke: Part 1 (13 studies)
Luke: Part 2 (14 studies)
Luke: Part 3 (12 studies)
The Servant King: A Study of the Gospel of Luke (10 studies)
El rey siervo: Un estudio sobre el evangelio de Lucas (en español, 10 estudios)
Romans, 2nd ed. (10 studies)
Galatians (8 studies)
Gálatas (en español, 8 estudios)
Philippians, 2nd ed. (10 studies)
Colossians (10 studies)

You can find all of our studies at athisfeetstudies.com.

About the Book Cover

All of the At His Feet Studies book covers are designed using the Greek or Hebrew letters of a word from the biblical text we're writing about.

In this study, we used the Hebrew word for *altar*, taken from multiple places in Haggai and Malachi. The design echoes the winged solar disc that appeared on Hebrew seals associated with the royal house of the Kingdom of Judah. Malachi 4:2 refers to the "sun of righteousness," which will rise with healing in its wings.